DRUGS AND THE LEGALIZATION DEBATE

The increasing rate of drug abuse by both teens and adults and the lack of success in stopping this abuse have led to a controversial debate about legalizing drugs.

DRUGS AND THE LEGALIZATION DEBATE

Jennifer Croft

THE ROSEN PUBLISHING GROUP, INC.
NEW YORK

Published in 1998, 2000 by The Rosen Publishing Group, Inc.
29 East 21st Street, New York, NY 10010

Revised Edition

Library of Congress Cataloging-in-Publication Data
Croft, Jennifer.
   Drugs and the legalization debate / Jennifer Croft.
     p. cm.— (The drug abuse prevention library)
   Includes bibliographical references and index.
   Summary: Discusses drug abuse and its penalties as well as the pros and cons of drug legalization.
   ISBN 0-8239-3206-0
   1. Drug abuse—United States—Prevention—Juvenile literature. 2. Drug abuse—Government policy—United States—Juvenile literature.
[1. Drug abuse. 2. Narcotics laws. 3. Drug legalization.] . I. Title. II. Series.
HV5809.5.C76   1997
362.29'0973—dc21   97-13948
                              CIP
                              AC

Manufactured in the United States of America

Contents

Introduction   *7*

Chapter 1   The Consequences of Drug Abuse   *11*

Chapter 2   Looking at Legalization   *19*

Chapter 3   The History of Drug Laws   *26*

Chapter 4   Zero Tolerance   *29*

Chapter 5   Exploring the Legalization Debate   *42*

Chapter 6   Drug Laws in Other Countries   48

Chapter 7   Asking Important Questions   51

Glossary   *57*

Where to Go for Help   *59*

For Further Reading   *61*

Index   *63*

The sale, manufacture, and use of cigarettes and other drugs, are controlled by the government.

Introduction

The discussion of current events in Mr. Duro's social studies class had never been so intense. The topic: Should drugs be legalized?

Raoul got the discussion started. "Humans have always used drugs," he said, "and they always will. Drug use is a matter of personal freedom," he continued. "Using drugs may be dangerous and deadly, but as long as you're hurting only yourself, it's a personal decision. No one has the right to tell you otherwise, and the government shouldn't be able to put you in jail for it. After all, many drugs are legal. Alcohol does a lot of damage, and its use is legal as long as you are twenty-one. Isn't this country supposed to be all about personal freedom and freedom of choice?"

Andrea jumped in. "Raoul's right," she said. "Until earlier this century, drug use and addiction was considered a medical problem, not a legal or criminal one—not something to put people in jail for. Even Coca Cola had cocaine in it."

"Besides," Dwayne added, "putting people in jail doesn't work. In the past twenty years in

8 | *this country, more people have been put in jail for drugs, for longer periods of time, than at any other point in history. The United States has more people in jail than any other nation in the world—and this is supposed to be the freest country on earth! A lot of those in jail are there for non-violent drug-related offenses."*

"But wait a minute," Kevin spoke up. "What you say may be true, but drugs harm families and neighborhoods, and frequently many innocent people get hurt."

"Yeah," Ana said. "What happens to kids whose parents are on drugs? Who's going to protect my sister when some smooth talker is after her and her friends to get high?"

Roberto said, "Isn't the government supposed to protect its citizens? How is it going to do that without making drugs illegal?"

The whole class was discussing both sides of the issue. Mr. Duro had to raise his voice to be heard. "Hey! That noise five minutes ago was the bell!" He was proud of his students. They were informed, and they were thinking. "To be continued," he called as the students filed out.

The Debate About Drug Legalization

Most drugs prohibited in the United States today were legal before 1914. Concerns about drug addiction and other factors led to the creation of drug laws.

These laws control the manufacture, sale, and use of all drugs. As illegal drug use has grown, some people have begun to wonder whether drug prohibition is really the best solution. Does making certain drugs illegal actually help solve the problem of drug abuse, or does it just make things worse? These questions have led many people to think about the advantages and disadvantages of the current drug policy in the United States.

In this book, we will explore the issues surrounding the drug legalization debate. We will try to answer the following questions: Does simply making drugs illegal really help to address some of the causes of drug use, such as poverty and hopelessness? What exactly is meant by drug legalization? Why are certain drugs illegal now? Why do some people believe that they should be legal?

There is no easy solution to the issue of drug legalization. That is why it may be difficult for you to determine which side you support. In this book, we will show both sides of the drug legalization debate. Once you have all the information, you can decide where you stand on the issue of drug legalization.

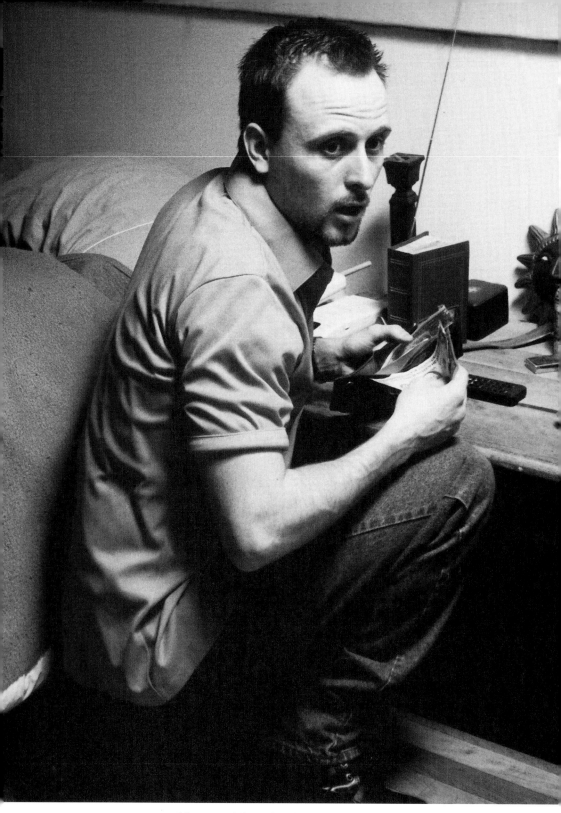

Some addicts steal from family and friends when they need money to buy drugs.

CHAPTER 1

The Consequences of Drug Abuse

*B*rian loved his uncle Jim. He never made Brian feel as though his problems didn't matter. Maybe because Jim was not Brian's dad, his immediate reaction wasn't to get angry when Brian came to him with a problem. Jim's own two daughters also adored their father.

Uncle Jim was a talented carpenter, but he had a cocaine problem. He also drank too much. Brian and his cousins couldn't stand to be around his uncle when he was high.

One Monday, Brian thought that the kids at school were acting strangely toward him. No one was talking to or even looking at him. It seemed as if everyone was avoiding him. His cousins were absent, too. Since it was a small school in a small town, Brian usually knew everything that was going on.

12 | *Finally his friend Kevin came up to him. "You all right, man?" Kevin asked.*

"Yeah," said Brian. "What's going on?"

"You don't know?"

"No, what? We were away all weekend."

"Mike Morlath was hit by a pickup truck and killed on Friday night."

"Oh my God," Brian said.

"That's not all," Kevin continued. "Your uncle was driving, Brian. He hit him, and he didn't stop. Someone saw the truck. The cops picked him up later. He was high, and the truck was smashed in. Brian started crying.

What Is Drug Abuse?

Before considering the issues involved in the drug legalization debate, it is important to understand the dangers of drug abuse.

Drug abuse—the harmful, nonmedical use of a drug—is a major problem. About 12 million Americans use illegal drugs.

If nobody abused drugs and if people used them only when they had a medical condition that required drug treatment, there would be no reason to prohibit drugs. However, many people do not take drugs just for medical reasons. They may take them to forget their problems or to try to feel good.

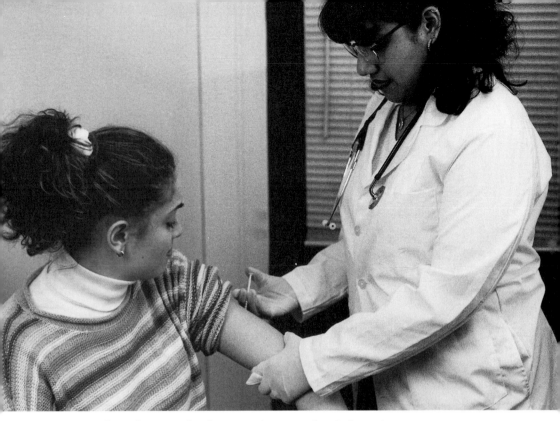

Some drugs have medical uses and are used to help patients with certain medical conditions.

Effects of Drugs

Drugs are substances that affect the body's functions. Drugs are not always bad. Many drugs have positive uses—they can save lives or help people to live free from pain. Such drugs are used as medicine. The aspirin you take when you have a headache is an example of a legal drug. However, drugs that have no accepted medical uses are illegal. But drugs, both legal and illegal, become a problem when people abuse them or become addicted to them. Addiction occurs when the user's

14 | body or mind becomes dependent on the drug.

Those who become addicted discover that it can be very hard to stop using. Users may stop caring about important parts of their lives, such as family and friends, their schoolwork, or their jobs. They may care only about the drugs they are addicted to. Even if they want to stop, they cannot. Many drugs are so addictive that users suffer physically and emotionally without them.

How Drug Abuse Affects Society

Year in, year out, public opinion polls indicate that Americans regard illegal drug use and criminal violence as the most important problems facing U.S. society. Many people believe that the problems are linked. Three million Americans are addicted to either cocaine or heroin, 50 million are addicted to nicotine, and 18 million are alcoholics. The following are just a few of the serious effects of widespread drug abuse:

• Violent crime has been linked to the drug trade and the use of illegal drugs. Drug-related violence and crime hurt many innocent people who get caught in the crossfire of gang wars or are robbed by addicts who want drug money.

- Drug abuse causes health problems. **15**
For example, the use of intravenous (IV)
drugs, like heroin, can increase a
person's chances of contracting HIV, the
virus that causes AIDS. Recent studies
indicate that intravenous drug use—
specifically, sharing needles—is the
leading cause of new HIV infections in
the United States.
- Drug abuse has a serious effect on
the economy. People who abuse drugs
cannot do their jobs well. Missing work
or making errors costs employers money.
This is especially true for people whose
work affects the safety of others, such as a
pilot or bus driver. When these people
make a mistake, they put people's lives at
risk. Also, a company can be sued if
someone gets hurt or killed because of a
mistake or an accident. When companies
must make up for the losses caused by
drug-abusing employees, they often cover
the cost by raising their prices. Indirectly
we all pay for drug abuse.

Drug Abuse and Teenagers

Drug abuse is an especially serious
problem among teenagers. The 1996
National Household Survey on Drug
Abuse found that 11 percent of

Some drug dealers use young teens to help them sell and distribute drugs.

American teens use drugs. In a 1995 study conducted by Columbia University's Center on Addiction and Substance abuse (CASA), teenagers said that the biggest concern in their lives is drugs.

Drugs are often easy to obtain in some neighborhoods and schools. A 1996 survey by the Partnership for a Drug-Free America found that half of all teenagers have been offered drugs, and about 38 percent of them have tried marijuana. Statistics also indicate that teenagers who smoke marijuana are much more likely to go on to use harder drugs, such as cocaine.

A 1995 study conducted by the University of Michigan found that almost half of high school seniors say they've tried illegal drugs.

Teens may become involved with gangs or petty crime to support their drug habits. They may not have the motivation to find good jobs or go to college after high school, choosing to make money by dealing drugs instead. Teens may be offered "easy money" to participate in drug dealing.

Drug dealers are using younger and younger teens to help them sell and

18 | distribute drugs. Dealers use young teens in the hopes that the police will not notice or suspect the teens because of their young age.

What Can We Do About Drug Abuse?
The U.S. government spends as much as $50 billion a year to stop the use of illegal drugs. This money pays for things like police patrols in neighborhoods where drugs are bought and sold, helicopters that watch for drug smuggling at our borders, and drug abuse awareness programs in schools.

Despite all of the money being put into anti-drug programs, the use of drugs has not fallen significantly since the "war on drugs" (stepping up efforts to stop illegal drug use) began under President Ronald Reagan in 1982.

Experts on both sides of the drug legalization debate agree that the drug problem is serious. But they have different opinions on how to solve it.

CHAPTER 2

Looking at Legalization

*D*rug legalization is an idea that has gained support among people of many different backgrounds and political beliefs. A growing number of people see some form of legalization as the best solution to the drug problem in the United States today. These people argue that current drug laws do not stop the problems of drug abuse and addiction. They believe that strict anti-drug laws actually cause more problems than they solve.

At the same time, there are many people who do not believe that drugs should be legal in any way. They think that the best way to fight drug abuse is to keep enforcing laws against drug use, sale, and possession. Many people believe that drug laws should be made even stricter and, in some cases, they have been.

Some legalization supporters believe doctors should be able to prescribe illegal drugs to people who are addicted to them.

What Does "Legalization" Mean?

Throughout this book, we use the term "legalization" very generally. The term "legalization" has come to include many different proposals to change current drug policies. There are many different proposals being discussed. Two people might agree that our drug policy needs to change, but their suggestions for changing it might be very different.

Legalization

Full legalization of drugs is a very extreme position. Few supporters of drug policy reform believe that all drugs should be legalized and sold in a free-market system like alcohol and tobacco.

There are many different types of legalization proposals. Most are referred to as "controlled legalization" to set them apart from the free-market approach.

Medicalization

Under medicalization, drug abuse is treated as a medical problem rather than as a criminal problem. Supporters of medicalization argue that doctors should be able to prescribe illegal drugs to people who are already addicted to them, and that treatment should be free and accessible to all. They believe that addicts who can receive drugs from their doctors will not commit crimes in order to support their habits. In addition, they claim that medicalization would help to ensure that addicts receive pure drugs and do not die from accidental overdoses.

Opponents of this proposal point out, however, that this method creates many problems. There is no guarantee that addicts who are provided with prescribed drugs will not sell their doses on the black market. Even if the addict were

One proposal of the harm reduction approach calls for increased drug education to discourage people from trying drugs.

forced to take the dosage at the doctor's
office, drugs like heroin would require
two daily visits. This would interfere with
the goal of helping addicts keep steady
jobs. Also, heroin addicts need to increase
their doses as they build tolerance.

Decriminalization

Under decriminalization, use and possession of a small amount of an illegal drug
is considered a civil offense (punishable
by a fine) rather than a criminal offense
(punishable by a jail sentence). One of
the advantages of decriminalization,
according to its supporters, is that it continues to discourage drug use. It also
frees up resources in the criminal justice
system, which would no longer have to
deal with arrests of casual drug users.

Opponents of decriminalization, however, point out that it does not address
the problem of drug dealers. They believe
that removing criminal penalties would
result in a higher demand for drugs while
allowing dealers to enjoy this increase in
income.

Harm Reduction

Supporters of harm reduction claim that
drug abuse is inevitable, that it is going to

In methadone clinics, the methadone is usually mixed with orange juice. Patients drink this mixture in the presence of a nurse or doctor.

happen no matter what. They argue that since society cannot stop drug abuse, it should do all it can to reduce its harmful effects, such as the spread of HIV. Harm reduction proposals often call for:

- increased drug education to discourage people from trying drugs,
- education for drug users on how to minimize the risks of drug use,
- and free and easily available maintenance and treatment programs for drug addicts.

Methadone Treatment: An Example of Harm Reduction

One kind of maintenance program used as an example by harm reduction supporters is methadone maintenance treatment for heroin addicts.

Methadone is a synthetic (human-made) opiate that is also addictive. It satisfies a heroin addict's craving without creating a "high."

Heroin addicts who use methadone do not have to suffer the withdrawal symptoms when trying to quit heroin. Many addicts are unable to cope with the withdrawal symptoms and eventually go back to using heroin. Users who take methadone have a better chance of quitting heroin for good and are often able to hold steady jobs and live normal lives.

Methadone programs are controversial, however. Some people feel that it is wrong to replace a heroin addiction with an addiction to methadone.

We have only mentioned a few of the many legalization proposals being discussed by supporters. Although they all support some form of legalization, they may not agree on one specific proposal.

CHAPTER 3

The History of Drug Laws

The Road to Drug Prohibition

Until 1914, it was legal under federal law to manufacture, sell, possess, and use the drugs that are illegal today. Opium (made from the juices of the poppy plant) was widely used in medicines throughout the nineteenth century. Morphine (a form of opium) and cocaine were also widely prescribed and used. Medicines containing these drugs were used to relieve pain and conditions, such as hay fever, insomnia (sleeplessness), and depression. This was before people realized how dangerous and addictive these drugs were.

Concern over the growing number of people becoming addicted to products containing certain drugs led to the Pure

Food and Drug Act of 1906. This law required that medicine labels specify whether drugs contained opiates or cocaine. Samuel Hopkins Adams, a journalist, played a part in the passage of the act by writing a series of articles about the medicine business. Adams tried to show that the public was not well-informed about the content of their medicines.

After the act was passed, sales of medicines containing opiates and cocaine dropped. Most Americans didn't want addictive substances in their medicines.

In 1914, President Woodrow Wilson signed the Harrison Narcotics Act into law, making narcotics illegal except for medical uses. Certain over-the-counter and mail-order medicines containing narcotics were still legal if the concentrations of the drugs were under certain limits.

In 1919, the Supreme Court determined that the Harrison Act made it illegal for doctors to prescribe narcotic drugs to addicts to maintain their addiction. The Supreme Court's decision reflected the public's reduced tolerance of drug addiction.

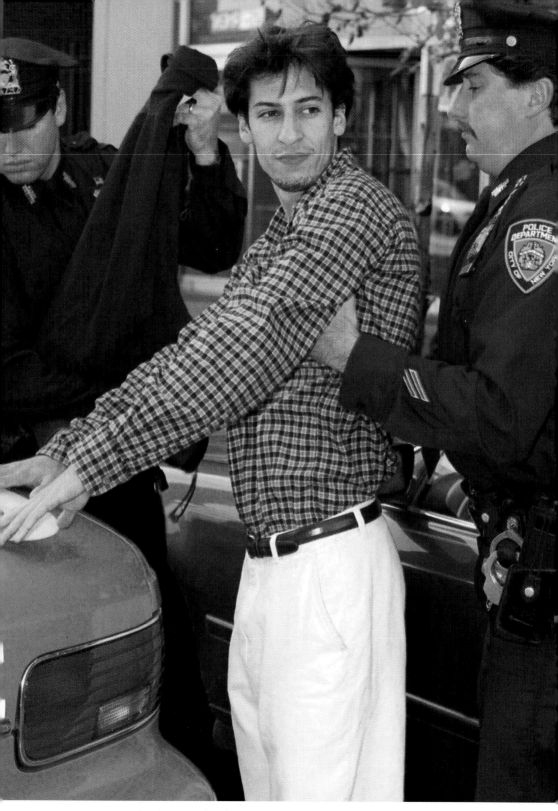

Enforcement of today's drug laws include arresting drug users and drug dealers.

CHAPTER 4

Zero Tolerance

*T*he discussion in Mr. Duro's class made Jill ask a lot of questions. She especially wondered about what Dwayne had said about jailing people for drugs. Was it true that the United States had more people in jail than anywhere else? Jill went to the library and did some research. What she discovered surprised her.

Dwayne was right. The United States has more prisoners in jail—a total of about two million at the end of 1999—than any other country. Although the United States prides itself on being the world's greatest democracy, Jill learned that it has half a million more prisoners in jail than China, which is often cited as the world's most repressive dictatorship. And China's population is more

30 *than four times greater than the United States! The rate of incarceration in the United States is four to six times higher than any country in Europe. California has more prisoners than the whole of western Europe.*

Most of these arrests had happened since 1980, Jill found out. Since that year, the prison population in the United States has quadrupled, driven by such tough crime measures as mandatory minimum sentencing and three-strikes-and-you're-out laws. A large percentage of those imprisoned since 1980 have been sentenced for nonviolent drug-related offenses. By 1995, fewer than one-third of those sentenced to prison were being punished for violent crimes. An estimated one-quarter of those jailed for drug offenses were sentenced for simple possession.

Jill knew that drugs were harmful, but she wondered if drug use was as damaging as putting such huge numbers of people in jail?

Why are some drugs legal and some not? Are legal drugs safer than illegal ones? These are some of the key questions in the drug legalization debate. We will take a look at both legal and illegal drugs and at the war on drugs, which focuses on illegal drugs.

Alcohol and Tobacco

Alcohol and tobacco are the two most common legal drugs. State laws regulate where and when alcohol can be sold. In a few towns, alcohol sale is illegal, but in most places it can be bought and consumed by people over age twenty-one.

Tobacco—usually sold in the form of cigarettes—can be legally purchased and used by persons over eighteen years of age. Federal law requires that tobacco products have a warning label that lists some of the health problems associated with the drug, including lung disease, cancer, and damage to babies if their mothers smoke while pregnant.

Even though they are legal, tobacco and alcohol are dangerous and even deadly drugs. According to the Centers for Disease Control and Prevention (CDC), one in five deaths is caused by tobacco use. There are three million smokers under the age of eighteen in the United States. Each year they purchase almost 950 packs of cigarettes, providing $1.2 billion in revenue for the tobacco industry. Even though the CDC calls smoking the most preventable cause of death in the United States, the number of teens who smoke daily doubled in the

32 | 1990s. The use of alcohol by teens also increased in the late 1990s. According to the National Institute on Drug Abuse, alcohol leads to increased injury and death from car accidents, difficulty in school, and legal problems. The driver is legally intoxicated in one-third of all fatal car wrecks. The younger an individual begins to use alcohol, the more likely he or she will be to have a problem with alcohol later in life. Likewise, teens who use tobacco are much more likely to use illegal drugs and drink heavily than their peers who do not smoke.

Other Legal Drugs

Prescription drugs are legal when properly prescribed, bought, and sold. When used correctly, they are helpful, but they can be dangerous if taken wrongfully or incorrectly. Some prescription drugs can also be addictive.

Household products such as glue and paint thinner, which are sometimes used as drugs, are not covered by drug laws. These drugs are called inhalants because users inhale their fumes to get high. Teenagers often experiment with inhalants because they are reasonably cheap and easy to obtain. However, just

Household products, such as glue, rubbing alcohol, and other substances that are sometimes used as drugs, are not covered by drug laws. However these products can be very dangerous.

because such products can be bought in supermarkets does not mean that they are harmless. Some household products are deadly when sniffed or "huffed." If they do not kill, they often cause major damage to young bodies and minds.

According to the Center for Substance Abuse Prevention, regular inhalant use can cause brain damage, violent behavior, and dangerous chemical imbalances.

Herbal formulas used for the purpose of getting high, such as "herbal ecstasy," are illegal in most states, even though

34 | they have, in some cases, been linked to injuries and deaths.

Caffeine is another legal drug. It is found in caffeinated beverages, such as colas, coffee, and tea, as well as in over-the-counter products designed to keep users alert and awake. Caffeine is addictive and can be harmful.

Why Are Some Drugs Illegal?

The government classifies drugs according to their "abuse potential"—that is, how likely they are to be used improperly or excessively.

Marijuana, heroin, LSD, and PCP are considered to have high abuse potential and are illegal in all circumstances. (Although in some states, marijuana laws have recently changed.) They can only be used for research on possible medical uses.

Cocaine, morphine, methadone, and amphetamines (drugs that speed up the body) are also believed to have high abuse potential, but they are considered to have some acceptable medical uses. These drugs can be prescribed, but only with nonrefillable prescriptions.

Barbiturates and codeine are considered to have abuse potential, but can be prescribed by doctors. They are usually

used as painkillers. Barbiturates and
codeine are depressants that slow the
body down.

Tranquilizers, such as valium and
Librium, are considered to have low
potential for abuse and acceptable medical
uses. This does not mean, however, that
they are not dangerous or addictive.

The "War on Drugs"

The current policy of the U.S. Government is to stop drug abuse through education and law enforcement. Two-thirds
of the federal drug budget goes toward
law enforcement. Law enforcement activities include arresting drug users and
dealers; patrolling our borders and seas to
stop drug smuggling; and stamping out
drug suppliers, such as marijuana growers
and illegal drug labs.

One of the major arguments used by
drug legalization supporters is that legalization would be less expensive to American citizens. They point out that the
government is spending billions of dollars
to fight illegal drugs. Police officers spend
much of their time making drug arrests.
More often than not, these arrests involve
small-scale users and dealers rather than
major drug suppliers and dealers.

36 Approximately 400,000 people are serving sentences for violating drug laws. That is one-quarter of the total prison population in the United States. More than 16,000 federal prisoners with no previous criminal history are serving an average of six-year sentences for breaking drug laws, according to a study by the U.S. Department of Justice.

Legalization supporters argue that taxpayers should not have to pay the costs of keeping drug law violators in jail and building new prisons.

Are We Fighting a Losing Battle?

Each year in the 1990s in the United States, between six and ten million arrests were made for drug-related offenses. Even so, the rate of drug use in the United States and the size of the illegal drug trade continues to climb. Though the government has stopped a lot of marijuana from entering the country, more people have started to grow their own.

The illegal drug trade is very difficult to stop simply because so many people are "addicted" to the huge amounts of money earned in smuggling and trafficking illegal drugs. The illegal drug trade generates an estimated $100 billion a year.

Ninety-eight metric tons of cocaine were seized by officials in 1995, but this amount was just a fraction of the cocaine used in the United States that year.

Many supporters of drug legalization argue that if drugs were legalized—if the manufacture, sale, and distribution of drugs were regulated by the government—there would be little reason for an illegal drug trade to exist. This would remove many of the dangers and violence associated with buying and selling drugs on the black market. Also, if the emphasis were on providing treatment for addicts rather than treating them as criminals, they would have a better chance of recovering from their addiction.

State Drug Laws

38

The same drugs are illegal in all fifty states but penalties for drug possession and distribution vary widely from state to state. This is especially true with marijuana. Even though growing or possessing any amount of marijuana is a crime under federal law, ten states (California, Colorado, Maine, Minnesota, Mississippi, Nebraska, New York, North Carolina, Ohio, and Oregon) have decriminalized personal possession of small amounts of marijuana. In these states, individuals possessing under a certain amount of marijuana are punished by a fine (usually about $100) rather than a jail sentence.

In 1996, voters in California and Arizona approved a law that allows doctors to prescribe marijuana. These laws are in direct conflict with federal law, however. The federal government has warned that doctors in Arizona and California who prescribe marijuana may have their prescription writing licenses taken away. They may even face criminal charges.

However, some doctors took legal action against the government. A judge ruled that the government can't take action against doctors in these two states for prescribing marijuana for medical purposes.

Do Some Drug Laws Go Too Far

Under federal forfeiture laws, any property can be forfeited (seized by the government) if it is "used or intended to be used" in a drug crime. Cars, homes, and even entire hotels and apartment buildings have been forfeited under these laws. Many people consider forfeiture laws unconstitutional (in violation of the U.S. Constitution).

Mandatory Minimum Sentencing

Jay was a high school senior who stayed out of trouble and hoped to go to college. He knew kids who partied and used drugs, but he stayed clean. "Where I'm from," he told his lawyers later, "everyone knows someone who's into drugs. That is just the way it is. If you have nothing to do with any of those people, you're gonna be one lonely dude."

Jay worked during the summers and on weekends. With some help from his mother, he was able to buy a car. He often drove his friends around. Sometimes they dropped off packages and received money in exchange, but Jay pretended he didn't notice. The less he knew the better, he figured. What he didn't know couldn't hurt him, right?

Wrong. Ultimately, four of Jay's friends were arrested and charged with conspiracy to

Under minimum sentencing laws, a person who makes the mistake of dealing, buying, or delivering drugs—even just one time—can be sent to prison for five years.

distribute crack cocaine. In exchange for pleading guilty to lesser charges, they agreed to testify against Jay, who they said was the driver for their criminal operation.

In his defense, Jay said that he had not known what his friends were doing, but the jury did not want to hear it. Jay was found guilty of conspiracy to distribute cocaine. Mandatory minimum sentencing laws gave the judge in the case no opportunity to go easy on Jay. His punishment: three life sentences. His friends all received much lighter sentences. One even got no time at all.

Another much-debated drug policy issue is mandatory minimum sentencing, which took effect as part of the Anti-Drug Abuse Act of 1986. Under mandatory minimum sentencing laws, drug offenders must serve a set number of years in prison based solely on the amount of the drug involved. For example, a person caught selling five or more grams of crack cocaine faces at least five years in prison. A person could also receive a five-year sentence for a crime involving one gram of LSD.

As a result of mandatory minimum sentencing laws, someone who makes the mistake of dealing, buying, delivering, drugs—even just one time—can end up in prison for five years. It doesn't matter what the circumstances are: If the person is found guilty, the law says that he or she must go to prison.

As we have discussed in this chapter, drug abuse is still a major problem despite the government's efforts. The next chapter will focus on the pros and cons of the legalization debate and will discuss whether legalization is the answer to the problem of illegal drugs.

CHAPTER 5

Exploring the Legalization Debate

*M*any people believe that it is time to start exploring new solutions to the drug problem in the United States. Some people believe that the answer is to make drug laws stricter. Others believe that drug laws are too strict already, and the solution is some form of drug legalization. Let's look at both sides of this debate.

Why Do Some People Support Drug Legalization?

The first thing to remember about drug legalization is that there are many different approaches and proposals for drug legalization. Individuals or organizations who agree that drugs should be legalized often have very different opinions on the details of a legalization plan.

Most supporters of drug legalization do not want drugs to be freely available to everyone. In fact, they feel strongly that drug abuse is a problem that is both dangerous for society and harmful for the abuser. But they also think that the current approach to the drug problem does not stop people from taking drugs. Most supporters of drug legalization support this approach because they believe that some form of legalization will eventually lead to less drug abuse.

But, you may be thinking, if drug legalization supporters agree that drug abuse is harmful, how can they possibly want to legalize drugs in any form? Let's look at some of the arguments used to support legalization.

• **Some illegal drugs may have medical uses.** Drug legalization supporters would argue that despite the potential of drugs to hurt people, they can also have some important medical uses. Supporters claim that cocaine, heroin, and marijuana can sometimes relieve pain for very sick people who are not helped by other drugs.
• **The government can't (and shouldn't) protect us from everything.**

44 Drug legalization supporters argue that many people engage in activities that are dangerous, such as skydiving, without the government's interference. Many people die every year from such activities yet they are perfectly legal. Diseases caused by drinking alcohol and smoking cigarettes kill many Americans, but smoking and drinking are legal for adults.

• **The war on drugs hurts more than it helps.** People who favor drug legalization often argue that the government's war against drugs is expensive, ineffective, and dangerous. It is impossible to keep drugs from getting into our country, they say. Fighting drugs like a war only encourages drug producers to fight back, sometimes violently.

• **The drugs produced by the black market can be deadly.** When drugs are unregulated, they can be impure and dangerous to users. Drug legalization would allow the government to regulate drug purity to reduce the risks of overdose and accidental death.

• **Legalizing drugs will bring in large amounts of useful tax money.** If drugs are legal, supporters of legalization argue, they can then be taxed, just like alcohol and tobacco. The money that will be gained by taxing drugs can be used toward drug abuse treatment and education.

Arguments Against Legalization

• **There would still be a black market for drugs among young people.** Drug legalization opponents, such as the Center on Addiction and Substance Abuse (CASA), believe that drug legalization would be disastrous. Illegal drug abuse today is mainly a problem for young people, and drugs would still be illegal to minors under most legalization proposals. Legalizing drugs for adults would still leave open the possibility of a huge black market for drugs to be sold to teenagers, opponents say.

• **Taxing drugs would encourage smuggling.** History professor David T. Courtwright points to the historical example of taxes on opium during the nineteenth and early twentieth centuries to show how taxing drugs would create more problems than it would solve.

At that time, the high taxes placed on opium led to violent criminal smuggling operations. Smugglers tried to get opium into the country without paying the high taxes.

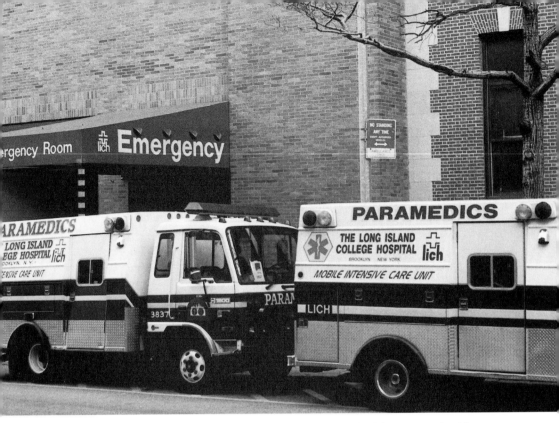

Because of the many people who have died because of addictions to legal drugs, such as alcohol and tobacco, many people are opposed to any legalization of illegal drugs.

• **There would be problems if drug laws varied from state to state.** Differences in state and national taxes and laws would lead to problems if drugs were legalized. What if one state charged higher taxes on drugs or enforced stricter laws than another state? This might encourage a criminal market in smuggling drugs from the lower-tax state into the higher-tax state. This illegal smuggling could lead to violent crimes.

• **Legalizing drugs would lead to more people using drugs—and more crime.** A 1995 paper published by

CASA claims that drug legalization would lead to an increase in crime committed by drug abusers. It states that certain drugs, such as cocaine, cause the user to become excited, irrational, and violent. More people using these drugs would mean more violent crimes.

• **Legalizing drugs would cause even more of the problems now caused by legal drugs.** The problems caused by addiction to legal drugs— primarily alcohol and tobacco—are frightening. Drunk drivers get into auto accidents; people who go to work drunk put themselves and their coworkers at risk; insurance and medical care costs go up because of the huge numbers of people suffering from alcohol and smoking-related illnesses. Assuming that legalizing drugs would increase the number of drug users, the cost to society could be enormous.

These are some of the major arguments used by both sides of the drug legalization debate. Both sides have some valid points. Let's look at examples of drug policies in other countries to give us an idea of what legalization might be like.

CHAPTER 6

Drug Laws in Other Countries

*D*rug abuse is an international problem. Some countries have drug laws that are even stricter than North American laws. In these countries, individuals found with drugs are immediately thrown in prison or even executed.

However, many European countries have adopted a "harm reduction" approach. In these countries, casual drug users are basically left alone, while addicts are treated as people with a medical problem rather than as criminals.

Addicts are provided with free treatment. In some cases, "maintenance" supplies of the drug to which they are addicted are provided so they will not have to commit crimes to support their habit. IV drug users are supplied with clean needles to reduce the risk of diseases being spread through infected needles.

The British Example

Great Britain responded to the problem of AIDS in the 1980s by allowing doctors to prescribe drugs, including heroin and cocaine, to addicts. Doctors prescribe oral dosages of the drugs. This method has brought down the number of injecting users and the rate of HIV infection in cities.

The programs adopted by these countries also raise many questions. Is it right for the government to pay (with taxpayers' money) for heroin and cocaine that are given to addicts? Should addicts be treated as sick people when taking drugs is a matter of personal choice?

The Swedish Example

Swedish policy originally favored drug harm reduction. Efforts were concentrated on major dealers, while users were basically left alone. Drug use, however, remained high, and many people began using heroin.

50   The government then changed its drug policy. Its goal became making Sweden a drug-free country. The government introduced the use of mandatory minimum sentencing laws. People caught with anything more than a marijuana joint were punished. In three years, arrests for drug offenses tripled. Drug use by young adults dropped drastically. In 1979, 37 percent of daily drug users were under the age of twenty-five. By 1992, only 10 percent were under twenty-five.

Different countries have different policies for dealing with their drug problems. The governments of some countries believe their societies will never be drug-free. They believe that since drug use is going to occur anyway, it should at least occur in a safer environment where addicts are given a chance to recover and become productive members of society again.

On the other hand, other countries disagree. They believe no drug use is acceptable unless it is for legal and accepted medical purposes. They will continue to put efforts into stopping all illegal drug use.

CHAPTER 7

Asking Important Questions

You have now had the chance to read about both sides of the drug legalization debate. We have examined the current and past drug policy in the United States, as well as drug policies in other countries. But there are still many important questions to be answered about this debate.

Would legalization cause more people to try drugs?

What if an adult could go to the drugstore and purchase almost any drug. Wouldn't he or she be at least tempted to try these drugs since there would be no risk of punishment?

Legalization opposers believe that legalizing drugs would encourage more people to try them.

Opponents of legalization argue that there are three main reasons why use would go up if drugs were legalized: availability, cost, and attitude.

First, if drugs are more readily available, more people will try them, legalization opponents argue. People who might not have known how or where to obtain drugs would suddenly have easy access to them.

Second, drugs will be cheaper if they are legal. Drug suppliers and dealers will not be marking up the prices to make their own profits. If drugs were more affordable, more people would try them.

Finally, opponents of legalization say $\quad$ **53**
that it is very important for the government to continue to take a stand against
drugs so that the public realizes that
they are harmful. They say that government tolerance of drugs sends a terrible
message. It will cause people to think that
drugs are not dangerous.

In response to the same question, supporters of legalization point out that even
though alcohol and tobacco are legal,
not everyone abuses them. Many people
choose not to drink or smoke at all. Many
others are able to do so occasionally without harming themselves or others.

Illegal drugs are fairly easy to obtain
already, say legalization supporters, yet
most people do not take them. Perhaps
more Americans would experiment with
drugs, supporters say, but this does not
necessarily mean that more Americans
would become drug addicts.

Many legalization proposals include
the possibility for addicts to receive
"treatment on demand." This means
treatment for drug addiction would be
free. Supporters of legalization claim that
even if legalization did result in a higher
number of people addicted to drugs,
treatment would be so much better and

so much more accessible under a system of legalization that these new abusers could have their addictions treated.

Opponents of legalization might argue that the main factor keeping people from trying drugs is that they are illegal. However, legalization supporters believe that personal and religious beliefs and fear of health risks are more likely to keep people from trying drugs. These beliefs and fears would still be in place if drugs were legalized.

What if legalization were a disaster?

What if the government decided to legalize drugs, and the situation got out of control? Imagine if millions of more Americans became addicted to drugs; if highway accidents skyrocketed because of the huge increase in drivers driving under the influence of drugs; if children were neglected as their parents turned to drugs; and if children turned to drugs themselves.

There's no way to predict what would happen if drugs were legalized.

Some opponents of legalization argue that it would be impossible to reverse a legalization policy once it were put in

Children of drug-addicted parents are often neglected or abused. Many legalization opposers fear that if drugs were legalized, more parents would become addicted and more children would suffer.

56 place. Legalizing drugs, and then outlawing them again, would make the problem even worse than before.

What are the chances that drugs will ever be legalized in the United States?

It doesn't seem likely to happen anytime soon. The majority of Americans are opposed to the idea of legalization. At the same time, other issues that have been raised in the legalization debate, such as needle exchange, methadone treatment, and mandatory minimum sentencing laws, may gain more attention. Even if it does not move in the direction of legalization, American drug policy may be pushed in a new direction. People who are tired of seeing their families, friends, neighborhoods, and communities ruined by drugs and drug-related crime want action taken to restore peace in their lives and communities.

As the legalization debate rages on—and as drug-related illness, crime, and violence rage on—it is likely that you will be faced with these questions in your future. They may even confront you as choices in the voting booth. How will you decide?

Glossary

accessible Easy to get ahold of; easily available.

addictive Term used to describe a substance (such as a drug) that causes users to become dependent on it.

AIDS (acquired immunodeficiency syndrome) An incurable disease of the human immune system that is transmitted through the exchange of bodily fluids.

black market Illegal trade in goods such as drugs.

decriminalize To make punishable by a fine rather than a criminal sentence.

enforcement Organized efforts to make people obey the law.

58 | **free market** Trade in legal goods.

HIV (human immunodeficiency virus) A virus that destroys cells in the immune system, leading to AIDS.

intravenous (IV) Occurring in or below the vein.

legalization The process of making something legal.

methadone A synthetic compound used to treat heroin addiction.

narcotics Drugs that dull the senses and put users into a stupor.

opiate Also called a narcotic; a drug that is derived from opium, a product of the poppy plant.

organized crime Criminal activities coordinated on a national or international scale.

over-the-counter Available without a prescription.

policy A course of action; usually used to describe a course of action taken by a government.

Prohibition The period from 1919 to 1933 when the manufacture, transportation, sale, and possession of alcoholic beverages was illegal in the United States.

smuggle To carry a certain product illegally from one place to another.

Where to Go For Help

IN THE UNITED STATES

Community Anti-Drug Coalitions of
   America (CADCA)
901 North Pitt Street, Suite 300
Alexandria, VA 22314
(703) 796-0560

Drug Abuse Resistance Education
   (DARE)
P.O. Box 2090
Los Angeles, CA 90051-0090
(800) 223-3273

Drug Policy Foundation
4455 Connecticut Avenue NW, Suite
   B-500
Washington, DC 20008-2302
(202) 537-5005
e-mail: dpf@dpf.org

Lindesmith Center
888 Seventh Avenue

60 | New York, NY 10106
(212) 887-0695
Web site: http://www.lindesmith.org
e-mail: lindesmith@sorosny.org

National Clearinghouse for Alcohol and
Drug Information
P.O. Box 2345
Rockville, MD 20847
(800) 729-6686
Web site: http://www.health.org

Parents' Resource Institute for Drug
Education (PRIDE)
100 Edgewood Avenue
Atlanta, GA 30303
(770) 458-9900
Web site: http://www.prideusa.org

IN CANADA

Addictions Foundation
1031 Portage Avenue
Winnipeg, Manitoba
R3G OR8
(204) 944-6200

Council on Drug Abuse
16 Scarlett Road
Toronto, Ontario
M6N 4K1
(416) 763-1491

For Further Reading

Baum, Dan. *Smoke and Mirrors: The War on Drugs and the Politics of Failure.* New York: Little, Brown and Co., 1998.

Duke, Steven B., and Albert C. Gross. *America's Longest War: Rethinking Our Tragic Crusade Against Drugs.* New York: Putnam, 1993.

Evans, Rod, and Irwin Berent. *Drug Legalization: For and Against.* La Salle, IL: Open Court, 1992.

Goode, Erich. *Between Politics and Reason: The Drug Legalization Debate.* New York: St. Martin's Press, 1998.

Inciardi, James A. *The Drug Legalization Debate.* Newbury Park, CA: Sage Publications, 1991.

Massing, Michael. *The Fix.* New York: Simon & Schuster, 1998.

Miller, Richard Lawrence. *The Case for Legalizing Drugs.* New York: Praeger, 1991.

62 | Oliver, Marilyn Tower. *Drugs: Should They
      Be Legalized?* Springfield, NJ: Enslow,
      1996.
  Schaler, Jeffrey A., ed. *Drugs: Should We
      Legalize, Decriminalize, or Deregulate?*
      Buffalo, NY: Prometheus Books, 1998.
  Terkel, Susan Neiburg. *The Drug Laws: A
      Time for Change?* Stamford, CT:
      Franklin Watts, 1997.
  Trebach, Arnold S. *Legalize It? Debating
      American Drug Policy.* Washington,
      DC: American University Press, 1993.

Index

A
Adams, Samuel Hopkins, 27
addiction, 14, 19, 26–27, 47
AIDS, 15, 49
alcohol, 7, 14, 21, 31–32, 44,
    47, 53
Anti-Drug Abuse Act (1986),
    41
aspirin, 13

B
black market, 21, 37, 44, 45

C
caffeine, 34
Center for Substance Abuse
    Prevention, 33
Center on Addiction and
    Substance Abuse
    (CASA), 17, 45, 47
cocaine, 14, 47, 49
Courtwright, David T., 45
crime, 14, 17, 45, 46, 47, 56

D
decriminalization, 23, 38
drug abuse, 12, 19, 43, 48
    definition of, 12–13
    effects on society, 14–15, 47
    teens and, 15–18
    treatment, 37, 45, 48, 53
    what you can do about, 18
drug laws, 9, 19

state, 38, 46
unconstitutional, 39
drugs
    abuse potential of, 34–35
    dealing, 17–18, 23, 35, 41,
        52
    ease in obtaining, 17
    education regarding, 24,
        35, 45
    effects of, 13–14
    intravenous, 15, 49
    medical uses of, 12–13,
        26–27, 34–35, 38, 43
    prescription, 32, 34, 38
    smuggling, 35, 36, 45
    tolerance to, 23

E
economic costs, 15, 18
ecstasy, herbal, 33–34

G
gangs, 14, 17

H
harm reduction, 23–25,
    48–49
Harrison Narcotics Act 1919,
    27
health problems, 15, 31, 48

heroin
    addiction to, 14, 25

64

medical prescriptions of,
    23, 43, 49
HIV, 15, 24, 49

I
illegal drug trade, 36–37
inhalants, 32–33

L
law enforcement, 35
LSD, 41

M
mandatory minimum
    sentencing, 41, 50, 56
marijuana, 17, 38, 43
medicalization, 21–23
medicine, 13, 26–27
methadone, 25, 56
morphine, 26

N
nicotine, 14

O
opium, 26, 45
overdosing, 21

P
Partnership for a Drug Free
    America, 17
prisons, 36, 41, 48
Prohibition (1919–1933), 9
Pure Food and Drug Act
    (1906), 26–27

R
Reagan, Ronald, 18

T
tax on drugs, 44, 45, 46
tobacco, 21, 31–32, 44, 47,
    53

U
U.S. Department of Justice,
    36
U.S. government, 18, 38–39,
    43–44, 53–54

W
war on drugs, 18, 30, 35, 44
Wilson, Woodrow, 27
withdrawal symptoms, 25

About the Author

Jennifer Croft is a freelance writer in New York City. She has written several books for young adults.

Photo Credits

cover photo by Sarah Freidman; p. 28 © A/P Wide World Photos; all other photos by Seth Dinnerman